# More Praise for *WillBe*

"Ian Ziskin's reputation and experiences in corporate America make this book a must read for those who aspire to be at the top, and those at the top who place bets on those who aspire to be there."

—Dennis Carey, Vice Chairman
Korn/Ferry International

"This is a high potential book—full of wisdom and practical advice that is within the grasp of anyone who truly desires to make a difference, and that's where it really begins, believing you make a difference! Don't be tempted to read this book quickly or all in one sitting—savor it, and really give some thought to the questions that Ziskin poses. This book raises the bar for every reader—*WannaBe*'s and *WillBe*'s alike. Make your own luck, read this book."

—Barry Z. Posner, Ph.D.
Coauthor, *The Leadership Challenge* and *The Truth About Leadership*

"Ziskin reminds us that the true secret to success lies in figuring out what we do best and doing it to the best of our ability. *WillBe* offers fabulous insights for anyone wanting to be the best person he or she can be."

—Randy Street
*New York Times* best selling author of *Who: The A Method for Hiring*
President, ghSMART & Co., Inc.

"*WillBe* captures the essence of successful attributes and behaviors that I have seen CEOs and other highly effective executives display throughout their careers. Ziskin presents them in a compelling, pragmatic, and understandable way that is extremely relevant to less experienced up-and-coming, aspiring leaders."

—Rick Smith, Founder and Former CEO, World 50
Bestselling author of *The Leap*

"*WillBe* is an extremely practical and fun read. Ian Ziskin is a guy who understands exactly what it takes to identify and develop up-and-coming talent."

—Rich Floersch, Executive Vice President, Human Resources
McDonald's

"Ziskin packs a lifetime of learning into this brief book—all you need to know about career success, pithily, even amusingly, presented. Buy it, read it, use it, and be a WillBe."
—Lee Dyer, Professor of Human Resource Studies
ILR School, Cornell University

"Ian Ziskin has distilled the insights of an exemplary career as an HR leader into a set of uniquely readable, direct, and useful guidelines for truly high potential leaders. These are the ideas you can draw upon every day."
—John Boudreau, Professor of Business and Research Director
Center for Effective Organizations
Marshall School of Business, University of Southern California
Author of *Retooling HR*

"Ian Ziskin has hit the mark with this wonderfully 'spot on' book on how to be a high performer in any organization. The frames and language Ziskin uses throughout the book stick with you from first glance, and the concepts stick just as easily. Based on years of experience as an HR guru and executive, Ziskin has created the equivalent of 'the little black book' for anyone wanting to succeed in life and organizations. Readers will find this book a helpful, useful, memorable tool that WillHelp you be a WillBe, not a WannaBe."
—Kimberly Jaussi, Ph.D.,
Associate Professor of Organizational Behavior and Leadership
School of Management, Binghamton University

"Advice about career building is offered by lots of self-styled experts, but it's rare indeed to have such advice provided by a senior human resources executive of major companies. Yet, Ian Ziskin knows his way around this subject intimately. He's produced a book that is not only filled with firing line-gained knowledge about career building, but also with specific action steps that people can take to make their careers successful. With a focus on key behaviors and related watchwords, Ziskin has produced a book about career building that is akin to Coach John Wooden's writings on leadership."
—David Lewin, Neil H. Jacoby Professor of Management,
Human Resources & Organizational Behavior
UCLA Anderson School of Management

"Succinct principles that are universally applicable to all leadership situations are hard to find. Ian Ziskin has captured highly meaningful leadership principles with practical examples to develop future and current leaders. This primer is an excellent contribution for leadership assessment and development."

—**Marcia Avedon, Ph.D., Senior Vice President,**
**Human Resources and Communications**
**Ingersoll Rand**

"Ian Ziskin has written a straightforward, provocative guide which can benefit all of us. It is a quick read . . . and a must read for anyone wanting to be the best he or she can be."

—**Tom Helfrich, Executive Vice President, Human Resources**
**KeyCorp**

"In *WillBe*, Ian Ziskin has coupled his years of leadership experience with his practical knowledge of effective organizational behavior, and applied them in a very readable set of examples. This tool kit of behaviors will assist anyone who works in any setting, where working effectively with others is important."

—**Curt Gray, Senior Vice President, Human Resources & Administration**
**BAE Systems Inc.**

"*WillBe* is a great read for self-motivated, early-in-career executives and managers who have aspirations to reach senior management. The 13-point checklist provides a simple and complete self-study guide to assess leadership potential and positively address skill gaps."

—**Greg Woodson, Vice President, Chief Ethics and Compliance Officer**
**Colgate Palmolive Company**

"Among my network members, the identification and development of high potential talent is an ever-present priority. Ian Ziskin's framework and guidance for high potential executives is a must read for current leaders looking to develop next generation talent, and for those who aspire to be leaders."

—**Mike Dulworth, President & CEO**
**Executive Networks, Inc.**

# WillBe

---

## 13 REASONS *WillBe*'s

## ARE LUCKIER THAN *WannaBe*'s

---

# Ian Ziskin

*Foreword by Dave Ulrich*

*WillBe: 13 Reasons WillBe's are Luckier than WannaBe's* makes a great gift, teaching tool, and/or self-help guide. For more information (including information on bulk purchases for friends, family, employees, or members of your group or organization) contact the author by email at info@exexgroup.com or visit the EXec EXcel Group LLC Web site at www.exexgroup.com.

Editing, design, and layout by Matt McGovern
www.700acres.com

# Table of Contents

*(continued)*

# Table of Contents

# Foreword

## "QUE SERA, SERA . . ."

*by Dave Ulrich*

THERE IS AN OSCAR winning song from the 1950s entitled, "Whatever Will Be Will Be (Que Sera, Sera)." The message of the song is that life gives us opportunities, and some take advantage of them and some do not.

This book is written for gifted individuals who want to take advantage of the opportunities given them.

Ian Ziskin is one of these talented individuals who accessed opportunities and turned them into achievements. I met Ian over 20 years ago when he was identified by a very wise Chief Human Resources Officer as one of the up and coming next generation HR leaders. With humility and drive, Ian fulfilled his potential and moved into CHRO roles where he influenced not only his company, but also the HR profession. He is uniquely positioned to observe how individuals live up to ("willbe") or live down to ("wannabe") their privileges.

While I knew of Ian's HR insights, his leadership ability, and his thought leadership, I was not aware that he is a marvelous writer. This book is not only perceptive, it is a fun read. The 13 behaviors and watchwords in his book target what aspiring leaders need to know and do. The case studies are captivating examples of what does and what does not work. I recognized many of the people (by action, not name) in the stories. Ian cleverly and clearly puts into words and cases what I have both seen and experienced. The self-diagnostics give the reader a quick mirror into what is or is not working.

Why should you read and use this book?

For some it is a reminder of what you intuitively know about moving forward in organizations (and in life, for that matter). It will reinforce your instincts and help make them patterns. Like the Boy Scout law ("a scout is trustworthy, loyal, helpful, friendly, courteous, kind, obedient, cheerful, thrifty, brave, clean, and reverent"), these 13 maxims could become the standard for aspiring leaders.

For some it is a guidebook that may shape how you respond to current and future work situations. You will likely face many of the situations Ian describes. Having anticipated and thought about your responses, you will more quickly demonstrate leadership maturity.

For some it is an after action review where you can figure out what may have (temporarily, we hope) derailed you. Ian describes failing forward when leaders learn from their mistakes.

All of the 13 principles are truisms that future or current leaders should understand and master. They have been talked about, researched, and applied in leadership literature for many decades. Ian does a masterful job of turning these maxims into actions. The simple test in the appendix can help an aspiring leader know where to focus attention to turn aspiration into reality.

I tried to pick my top three of the 13 reasons and found it impossible. All 13 behaviors and watchwords matter. In our work on leadership in *The Leadership Code,* we describe personal proficiency at the heart of successful leadership. These 13 ideas elegantly define personal proficiency. From ethics to execution, leaders who are conscious of how their behavior impacts others will be more likely to succeed.

Que sera, sera (whatever will be will be) is not a random walk through the corridors of organization leadership opportunities. The *WillBe's* intentionally take care of themselves to navigate the leadership maze with the personal proficiency required to succeed over time. This book is both a compass that gives future leaders a direction and a map that offers specific turns for their leadership success.

—  Dave Ulrich, Professor of Business,
    Ross School of Business, University of Michigan
    Author of more than 20 books, including *The Why of Work*
    Cofounder of The RBL Group

# Dedication

THIS BOOK IS DEDICATED to my *WillBe's*—my sons Tyler, Eric, and Matthew—and to their mother and my wife, Susan Edwards, who has helped make them so.

*"Don't measure yourself by what you have accomplished, but by what you should have accomplished with your ability." – Coach John Wooden*

# Introduction

THIS BOOK WAS STARTED nearly 53 years ago, even though I have actually only been writing it for the past 18 months. It is a product of feelings, thoughts, and experiences that have evolved over a lifetime of learning, doing, learning, doing.

The feelings have been about spending time with the people I love, doing the things I love.

The thoughts have been about how to be the best person I can, and how to help others be their best.

The experiences have been about the successes and failures that shape me—indeed all of us—tempered by a sense of humility and humor.

The premise of this book is simple . . . everyone has talent and potential, but not everyone will be equally successful at realizing his or her full potential. Not everyone is a "WillBe." But you could be.

I suppose I might have called this book *CouldBe,* but I have more confidence in you than that. *WillBe* takes a decidedly more optimistic tone than *CouldBe!*

So, how do you know where you stand, and how do others tell the difference between you and everyone else?

*WillBe's* are high potentials who have the promise and ability to take on positions of additional responsibility and accountability over time, and to perform at levels that far exceed others. They clearly have what it takes—the ambition and attributes, the will and the skill—to fulfill the promise that others see in them.

In contrast, *WannaBe's* may aspire to achieve great things and to live up to lofty expectations, but they do not have what it takes.

This book is about distinguishing the *WillBe's* from the *WannaBe's*.

There has been a considerable body of literature published over the years on leadership and leadership development. *WillBe* is not really about either one. It is about discovering, identifying, and nurturing high potential talent—before they ever assume senior level leadership positions—and understanding what makes them *WillBe's* in the first place.

I have written this book for you, the aspiring WillBe, to provide some insight into what highly talented and successful people actually do and how they behave early in their careers when their operating styles and reputations are still forming and evolving.

- Are you getting ready to complete college or graduate school?
- Are you in the first 10-15 years of your career?
- Do you aspire to realize your full potential?

*WillBe* may help you figure out how to conduct yourself so you will achieve greater success.

The book offers some perspectives and lessons learned that are intended to improve your chances of being seen as a WillBe, fulfilling the expectations that others have of you, and living up to the high expectations that you should have of yourself.

Are you a WillBe or a WannaBe? Are you sure?

*WillBe* summarizes 13 things truly successful high potentials do extremely well, behaviors others see them exhibiting very early in their careers. These things are what get them noticed and cause other people to believe in them. Displaying these behaviors, consciously or unconsciously, is what makes them *WillBe's* and separates them from the *WannaBe's*.

Some readers might think that 13 is a rather "unlucky" number to use when describing what highly successful up-and-comers do. However, the success of *WillBe's* has a lot less to do with luck than it has to do with great capabilities and preparation. Seneca, the Roman dramatist, philosopher, and politician, was onto something when he said, "Luck is when preparation meets opportunity."

It's often said that, "It's better to be lucky than good." *WillBe's* are better than lucky.

This book is based on behaviors that I have consistently seen in action over nearly 30 years of experience working with and developing thousands of up-and-coming leaders across multiple industries. The 13 dimensions highlighted herein are not intended to be exhaustive or definitive. You may find other things helpful in determining whether you are a WillBe or not. I simply offer these insights as a pragmatic list based on my experience.

While *WillBe* is written from the perspective of the business environment, the lessons and themes have direct applicability to understanding successful high potential talent in any organization including academic, business, military, political, religious, or social. It will be gratifying to me if this book proves helpful to leaders, managers, mentors, teachers, coaches, consultants, and family and friends who believe in the importance of identifying and developing *WillBe's*. But I did not write this book for them.

*WillBe* is for you. It's only 117 pages for a reason: so you can quickly find something useful and return to your busy WillBe life. Use the self-assessments to learn more about yourself, better understand your strengths and weaknesses, and identify actions you will take as a result.

Comments, questions, and stories of your triumphs and challenges are most welcome. Please contact me at info@exexgroup.com. Enjoy!

–   Ian Ziskin
    January 2011
    Calabasas, California

# Chapter 1

## DEFINE THE MOMENTS

### *Watchword:* Ethics

SOMEONE ONCE TOLD ME, "You never know what your values are until they cost you something." This philosophy is a great way of underscoring the importance of an unwavering commitment to ethics and integrity, even if it's inconvenient or messy. No compromises. No shortcuts. No excuses. No kidding.

True *WillBe*'s seem to understand that the highest standards of ethics and integrity are foundational to everything else. High potentials will not be viewed as such without also being seen as high integrity people. They cannot maintain the highest ethical standards unless they are prepared to raise issues, ask tough questions, take a stand, and potentially put themselves at risk by irritating people who may not like being questioned or second-guessed. This capability is particularly important for *WillBe*'s who often do not yet hold positions of power in their organizations. Confronting ethical dilemmas can be uncomfortable, but it must be done when circumstances call for it.

*WillBe*'s know how to push back and challenge things that seem unethical, without offending people unnecessarily or seeming like alarmists or holier than thou. It's a delicate balance, but these kinds of dilemmas are what I mean by **Define the Moments**. How these situations are handled can shape one's reputation for years to come. Ethical choices are not about doing what's convenient or safe; they are about doing what's right. At one of my previous employers, we called this behavior "know when to challenge and when to support."

## A Situation!

Steve and Dana are Division General Manager and Deputy General Manager, respectively, of a large manufacturing division. They receive an urgent call from the company's "Ethics Open Line" indicating that a sexual harassment complaint has been filed against one of the division's plant managers.

This plant manager has been in his role for about six months. By all accounts, he has done an excellent job turning around the plant, which previously had a series of quality, delivery, and financial problems. He has been with the company for 25 years, and was transferred into this job from another plant because of his skill fixing troubled businesses and his positive relationship with the plant's most important customer.

Following a thorough investigation by the Human Resources and Law Departments, Steve and Dana learn that the plant manager has been accused by a temporary contract employee of making repeated inappropriate and unwanted sexual advances. In addition, he is accused of following the contract employee around town on several occasions (what she describes as "stalking her") in an attempt to watch her, touch her inappropriately, and ask her out on dates. The temporary employee asked the plant manager repeatedly to discontinue his behavior, but to no avail. She then filed the complaint.

The investigation has revealed that the plant manager did in fact repeatedly approach the employee to discuss his sexual interest in her. In addition, he followed her in his car as she drove to her home and around the small town where they and their families live. The plant manager has admitted he did the things of which he has been accused, but maintains he meant no harm, has genuine feelings for the employee, and isn't really sure why he decided to follow her around town.

Steve and Dana believe something must be done about the plant manager's behavior, and they discuss the issues and alternatives with their heads of HR and Law. Steve acknowledges that the plant manager must be disciplined, but he is very concerned that firing him would be extremely disruptive to the plant's performance and recent recovery, and would therefore jeopardize the division's operating and financial performance. Steve is also worried about the key customer's reaction if the plant manager were to be terminated. Dana thinks that, despite the risks associated with firing the plant manager, failure to do so would be seen by employees as "looking the other way" in handling a very serious violation of the company's values, ethical standards, and policies.

Steve and Dana approach you for your input. What do you tell them?

## Notes

_____

_____

_____

_____

_____

_____

_____

_____

_____

_____

_____

_____

## Handling this Situation!

If the first thing that pops into your mind about Steve and Dana's dilemma is how inconvenient it would be to fire the plant manager, you are focused on the wrong thing. Don't gloss over a question of ethics. Get the facts and make sure the right people are involved in any investigation. Advocate discipline that is reasonable for the ethical offense committed. Even give people a second chance if the situation and the offender's reputation warrant it.

But once a determination has been made regarding the appropriate actions to be taken, take them. Make it clear that you are not willing to sacrifice your reputation for someone else's convenience. In this case, the plant manager needs to go.

### Some additional advice for *WillBe*'s about Ethics . . .

- Challenge up the organization to superiors whenever ethical questions arise, and support down in the organization to protect and encourage those who may be reluctant to raise such issues.

- Foster confidential means for people to express their ethical concerns.

- Never ask anyone to do something you wouldn't do yourself.

- Insist on the highest standards of personal ethics and integrity for yourself, and make it clear that you expect no less from others.

- Safeguard your reputation; it takes a lifetime to build and only a moment to destroy.

## Self-Assessment

Mark the column that best describes your situation today.

| *Do I . . .* | Strength | Weakness | Not Sure |
|---|---|---|---|
| Challenge up and support down? | ———— | ———— | ———— |
| Foster confidentiality? | ———— | ———— | ———— |
| Only ask others to do what I would do myself? | ———— | ———— | ———— |
| Insist on the highest ethics? | ———— | ———— | ———— |
| Safeguard my reputation? | ———— | ———— | ———— |

## Actions I Will Take to Build on a Strength, Improve on a Weakness, and/or Learn More about Myself

_____

_____

_____

_____

_____

_____

_____

_____

_____

_____

_____

# Chapter 2

## DO UNTO OTHERS

### *Watchword:* Respect

W*ILLBE'S* ARE OFTEN SMARTER, more capable, and more likely to move ahead quickly in their organizations than their peers and bosses. Sometimes, they know it and make sure everyone else knows it too! This dynamic presents some interesting challenges to interpersonal chemistry between *WillBe's* and the people around them. Casey Stengel, the legendary baseball manager, said, "The secret of leadership is to keep those who don't like you away from those who haven't made up their minds." That's sage advice for *WillBe's*, too.

While *WillBe's* have a lot of cheerleaders and people who want to take credit for their success, there are also plenty of people who would like nothing better than to see them fail. Petty jealousies and an overly competitive spirit can cause certain individuals to do nasty things. Yet *WillBe's* have an uncanny ability to operate above the fray by endearing themselves to others who have no particular reason to want to help them.

There is not really any rocket science to this phenomenon. Well-regarded *WillBe's* simply know how to treat other people with dignity and respect. They live by the golden rule and **Do Unto Others** as they would have done unto them.

The most successful *WillBe's* do not focus on how smart they are, or what position they hold relative to others. They behave as if they have something to learn from everyone and treat people well because they value them as people—no matter whether those people can help them get ahead or not.

## A Situation!

Kim and Monique are extremely intelligent high potentials who graduated last year with MBAs from prestigious universities. In addition to being incredibly smart, they are hard working, highly motivated, creative, and dedicated. They are thrilled to be among the first participants in the new two-year rotational development program called "STAR," which stands for "Super Talented, Always Right."

The STAR program is a wonderful way to get broad experience and exposure across the company's businesses, functional disciplines, and geographic locations—not to mention high visibility with very senior leaders. But as the saying goes, "There is a fine line between visibility and notoriety." If participants do well in the STAR program, everyone knows it. If they don't do well, everyone knows that, too.

Despite the intense pressure and bright lights of being a STAR, Monique has managed to excel and endear herself to just about everyone. She is considered a pleasure to work with and highly competent. Kim is also well-regarded in many ways, but has managed to alienate quite a few people, especially those she sees as beneath her in the organizational hierarchy. For example, her reputation among the administrative assistants—who talk quite candidly and regularly—is not very positive. Kim is seen as condescending, dismissive, and rude.

You have a close working relationship with one of the informal leaders among the administrative assistants who tells you that he wants to talk to you privately about some issues involving Kim and Monique since you oversee the STAR program. The administrative assistant proceeds to tell you about the contrasting views of Kim and Monique, the damage Kim's approach is doing to her reputation, and how well regarded Monique is.

He then asks you to give Monique some positive feedback on behalf of the appreciative administrative assistants, and to talk to Kim about her negative behavior—since few people other than you want to see her succeed. What will you say to each of them?

## Notes

_____

_____

_____

_____

_____

_____

_____

_____

_____

_____

_____

## Handling this Situation!

Kim and Monique are very representative of many extremely bright and capable up-and-comers. They both have terrific attributes and potential, but don't share the same approach to dealing with people, particularly with those who are less senior in the organizational hierarchy.

The conversation with Monique is a happy one: "You are very well regarded, and are managing to earn the respect of all kinds of people, including the administrative assistants. By the way, it's great to have them on your side, because they can make your life very easy if they want to and totally miserable if they don't. Respect begets respect."

The conversation with Kim is almost exactly the same, except for the part about earning the respect of the administrative assistants. That part of the conversation needs to be constructive, but brutally candid: "You are managing to really turn off the administrative assistants as a result of your rude and condescending attitude and comments. Treat them the same way you treat people in the organization you think are important—because they are important."

........................................................................................................................................

**Some additional advice for *WillBe*'s about Respect . . .**

- Treat everyone as you wish to be treated, and as you want people you care about to be treated.

- Never compromise the dignity of another human being.

- Say "please" and "thank you," especially when you don't have to.

- Praise publicly; criticize privately and constructively.

- Apologize *and* mean it.

........................................................................................................................................

## Self-Assessment

Mark the column that best describes your situation today.

| *Do I . . .* | Strength | Weakness | Not Sure |
|---|---|---|---|
| Treat everyone as I wish to be treated? | ___ | ___ | ___ |
| Never compromise dignity? | ___ | ___ | ___ |
| Say please and thank you? | ___ | ___ | ___ |
| Praise publicly and criticize privately? | ___ | ___ | ___ |
| Apologize *and* mean it? | ___ | ___ | ___ |

## Actions I Will Take to Build on a Strength, Improve on a Weakness, and/or Learn More about Myself

_____

_____

_____

_____

_____

_____

_____

_____

_____

_____

_____

_____

_____

# Chapter 3

## SHOW AND TELL

*Watchword:* Credibility

BARRY POSNER AND JIM Kouzes, coauthors of great leadership books such as *Credibility* and *The Leadership Challenge*, talk about credibility in terms of "DWYSYWD" (Do What You Say You Will Do). *WillBe*'s build credibility very early in their personal lives and careers. They show they are credible by telling people what they are going to do, doing it, and then showing people once again that they actually did it. Life is **Show and Tell**.

Despite being credible, however, successful *WillBe*'s are not perfect. They make mistakes just like everyone else. What distinguishes them is the way they handle their mistakes.

*WillBe*'s are quick to acknowledge and own up to their mistakes. They identify the problem, fix it, and avoid making lame excuses or blaming others.

*WillBe*'s display maturity early in their lives, and turn mistakes into opportunities to impress. They recognize that effectively resolving their mistakes often breeds more credibility than if they never made a mistake in the first place.

*WillBe*'s also know how to handle personal, private, and confidential information discreetly. They do not violate trust by blabbing everything they know, nor do they spread rumors—especially the hurtful kind. They leave those misguided actions to the *WannaBe's*.

## A Situation!

Ali and Michael are co-leading a project team of highly engaged engineering, finance, and marketing people who are working on a new product launch. This is their first time running a project of this size, scope, and importance. Everyone is watching, not only how the new product will do, but how Ali and Michael perform as leaders.

Deadlines are tight, resources are limited, and the team has been working many late nights and weekends. They are scrambling to bring the project in on time and within budget, while simultaneously delivering a technical solution that will wow senior leadership and the customer.

Finally, the big day arrives. It's time to present the new product concept, marketing plan, and financial projections to the senior leadership team. Ali and Michael are exhausted but confident. As a reward for their team's great work, Ali and Michael have invited their heads of engineering, finance, and marketing to attend the meeting to get some visibility with senior leadership.

Ali and Michael begin the presentation and make it to the second PowerPoint chart (the first one is the cover page). The chief financial officer then goes on the attack. He isn't even listening to the presentation because he has already skipped ahead to page 26 of the presentation, which addresses the financial projections including operating margin, return on investment, and cash flow. He tells the team, "These numbers are all screwed up."

The chief marketing officer then jumps in, criticizing the market share projections on page 12. "I don't understand where some of these assumptions came from," she says.

Michael immediately begins to backpedal, turns to the project team's finance and marketing people and says, "You two have really let me down.

You never should have given me numbers that were not correct. It's not my fault if you didn't do your homework."

Ali interrupts as quickly as he can and says to the CFO and CMO, "To the extent any of our numbers are not correct, I take full responsibility as the co-leader of this team. That said, our team has worked very hard on this analysis and I believe we will be able to answer any specific questions or concerns you may have during this meeting. If there are any remaining issues by the time we are finished today, you have our team's commitment to address and resolve them within one week."

Although the CFO and CMO don't win any congeniality awards, the meeting concludes two hours later with four of six issues clarified and resolved. The remaining two open issues have action plans identified for follow-up.

You are one of the participants in the meeting. Ali and Michael come to you to discuss post-meeting lessons learned on how they handled things and what they might have done differently. What suggestions do you give them?

## Notes

_____

_____

_____

_____

_____

_____

_____

_____

_____

_____

## Handling this Situation!

It would be a good idea for Ali and Michael to pre-brief the CFO and CMO on the presentation data to ensure people are on the same page heading into the meeting. One's credibility is rarely enhanced via the element of surprise, especially when the surprise is negative or not well understood.

Nevertheless, Ali does a nice job of taking responsibility for any disagreements or misunderstandings, and commits to make things right—either during the meeting or shortly thereafter. While that approach likely helps Ali's credibility with the CFO and CMO, perhaps more importantly, it solidifies credibility with the project team because he takes the heat on their behalf.

Michael, on the other hand, makes a major blunder, which is blaming members of the team in a public forum without even knowing if they actually did something wrong. Further, even if they did make mistakes, throwing your team under a bus to make yourself look better is inexcusable. Period.

---

### Some additional advice for *WillBe*'s about Credibility . . .

- Do what you say you will do.
- Take personal responsibility and accountability; don't make lame excuses or blame others.
- When you make a mistake or create a problem, admit it, fix it, and move on.
- Know what you don't know.
- Keep confidential information confidential.

---

## Self-Assessment

Mark the column that best describes your situation today.

| *Do I . . .* | Strength | Weakness | Not Sure |
|---|---|---|---|
| Do what I say I will do? | _____ | _____ | _____ |
| Take personal responsibility? | _____ | _____ | _____ |
| Admit and fix my mistakes? | _____ | _____ | _____ |
| Know what I don't know? | _____ | _____ | _____ |
| Keep information confidential? | _____ | _____ | _____ |

## Actions I Will Take to Build on a Strength, Improve on a Weakness, and/or Learn More about Myself

_____

_____

_____

_____

_____

_____

_____

_____

_____

_____

_____

_____

_____

_____

# Chapter 4

## BRING OUT THE BEST

### *Watchword:* Leadership

I HAVE BEEN AROUND all kinds of leaders in my life, both highly effective and ineffective. They come in all shapes and sizes. They have different strengths, weaknesses, and operating styles. I have also read hundreds of books and articles on leadership, all with their own ways of dissecting and characterizing leaders. There are endless ways to describe what great leaders do and don't do, and what poor leaders should and shouldn't do.

In my experience, one universal theme rings true about extremely effective leaders. They **Bring Out the Best** in people, even under the most unexpected circumstances. This realization is summed up for me with a line from the movie, *As Good as it Gets*. Jack Nicholson's character, Melvin Udall, says to Helen Hunt's character, Carol Connelly, "You make me want to be a better man."

Whether the setting is work, family, sports, music, theatre, school, military, community, politics, or religion, great leaders cause other people around them to be better—and they surround themselves with the very best people they can find. Even highly talented people become more confident, effective, and engaged. Good people gravitate to strong leaders, wanting to be around them, aspiring to live up to their higher standards and expectations.

*WillBe's* display these leadership qualities early in their lives and careers, even before they assume formal positions of leadership. Other people seem to feel and perform better as a result of being around *WillBe's*. *WillBe's* generate positive energy and have a hard-to-explain multiplier effect on other people's capabilities and commitment.

## A Situation!

Maria and Raj are both high potential leaders with strong records of delivering results. They know one another, but currently work in different operating divisions. Maria's business has grown significantly over the past few years and senior management has decided to split the business in half.

While disappointed to lose some of her business's key people and products, Maria is very supportive of the decision because she understands the strategic rationale for the split. Maria's boss has selected Raj to run the other half of the business.

Maria has a reputation for being a very involved, caring, engaging, and inspirational leader. People love working with and for her. They see her as a great listener who surrounds herself with very talented people whom she lets do their jobs—and she delivers great results.

Raj also delivers great results, but many people believe that is where the similarity between Maria and Raj ends. Raj is known as a micromanaging control freak. He has very specific and inflexible ways of operating and prefers to surround himself with team members who do things his way. Most people do not like working with or for him. Management—even Maria—seems to be blind to Raj's shortcomings, perhaps because he has delivered strong results consistently in the past. Of course, Raj is unaware of how he is viewed.

Within minutes of the announcement detailing the organization split and Raj's appointment, the hallways and chat rooms are abuzz. The employees who will remain working for Maria are dancing in their cubicles. Those who will be working for Raj begin updating their resumes.

Unfortunately, Raj lives down to his reputation. He proves to be very focused on business results without a complementary focus on people. He excels at telling people what to do, but is not very good at causing employees to feel valued, nor is he skilled at building commitment and enthusiasm. Within six months, voluntary attrition in Raj's new organization spikes by 30%, 15 key openings in the sales and strategy functions remain unfilled, and workforce engagement scores are trending downward.

Both Raj and Maria are alarmed by these negative results. After spending considerable time debating the root causes, they come to you for your objective insights. What do you say?

## Notes

_____

_____

_____

_____

_____

_____

_____

_____

_____

_____

_____

_____

_____

_____

_____

_____

## Handling this Situation!

Although Maria may not have been aware of Raj's negative reputation before, she most likely is now. She is probably trying to minimize damage to the business and people that used to report to her, even more than she is interested in helping Raj. Whatever her motivation, Raj needs support in several forms—feedback on how he is viewed, coaching on how to utilize and listen to his key people better, and help in articulating his leadership philosophy and communicating it throughout his organization. He also needs to identify the 20% of his people who matter most to the success of the business and begin spending time with them, seeking their ideas, and making them feel valued. If you think it will be difficult to get Raj to change, despite the mounting evidence, you are right. He probably has not received much negative feedback in the past.

### Some additional advice for *WillBe*'s about Leadership . . .

- Act like a leader before you become one; it takes practice.
- Have a personal leadership philosophy and tell people what you stand for.
- Surround yourself with the very best people, and rely on, listen to, and fully utilize them.
- Show people that you care about them as people.
- Push back on things that don't make sense and push forward on things that do.

## Self-Assessment

Mark the column that best describes your situation today.

| *Do I . . .* | Strength | Weakness | Not Sure |
|---|---|---|---|
| Act like a leader? | ——— | ——— | ——— |
| Have a personal leadership philosophy? | ——— | ——— | ——— |
| Surround myself with the best people? | ——— | ——— | ——— |
| Show people I care about them? | ——— | ——— | ——— |
| Push back and push forward? | ——— | ——— | ——— |

## Actions I Will Take to Build on a Strength, Improve on a Weakness, and/or Learn More about Myself

_____

_____

_____

_____

_____

_____

_____

_____

_____

_____

_____

_____

# Chapter 5

## PLAY SANDBOX

*Watchword:* Collaboration

WATCHING CHILDREN PLAY IN a sandbox is the best way I know to understand collaboration in organizations. Some kids share their toys willingly, and even seem to enjoy doing so. Others not only hoard their own toys, but try to steal everyone else's stuff, too.

The kids who share tend to attract other kids who also share, and they all have fun together. The kids who don't share often get ostracized, or worse, smacked in the head with a shovel or pail.

*WillBe's* **Play Sandbox** by willingly sharing ideas, resources, and people. They reach out to others across organizational boundaries. They work and play well with others. They don't grab toys that don't belong to them.

When inevitable disputes arise, *WillBe's* create win-win solutions, and they resolve conflicts without running to Mommy or Daddy to tattletale. They make great teammates.

*WillBe's* also understand that one of the greatest ironies about collaborative organizations and people is that they embrace constructive conflict. They recognize that collaboration is not only about working together to reach agreement, it's also about learning how to manage and capitalize on disagreement.

## A Situation!

Dontrelle and Danielle are very good friends at work as well as on a personal basis. They have worked together for five years and have had many discussions about their hopes, dreams, and aspirations for their careers and families. They are both high energy and ambitious people, and when they are together, they love to talk about organizational politics and who hates whom. When they are apart, sometimes they can't help talking about one another—occasionally in unflattering ways.

In addition to being colleagues and friends, they are both being considered for a promotion to the same highly coveted position. In an effort to decide which of these two well-regarded people to promote, the senior vice president gives them the same special assignment—develop a plan to revitalize the business unit they will be running if promoted. Everyone knows about this assignment and is looking forward to seeing how Dontrelle and Danielle approach it.

Ostensibly, the assignment will showcase their individual talents and operating styles. In reality, the job for which they are competing requires extraordinary collaboration skills. Therefore, the senior vice president wants to see if Dontrelle and Danielle conclude that, for best results on this particular assignment, working together will yield a better overall outcome for the business than competing with one another.

During the first two weeks of this six-week project, Dontrelle and Danielle maintain their friendly relationship, but restrict their conversations to overall company topics and family news. They do not discuss the special assignment at all, and work completely independently.

In the third week of the project, Dontrelle approaches Danielle about working together to brainstorm ideas for several key issues related to the special project. Danielle's response is a polite, but cool, "No thanks."

Two days later, Dontrelle sends Danielle an email outlining a few ideas and asks for her input. Danielle is on the email distribution list along with six other people from whom Dontrelle wants to solicit suggestions. Not only does Danielle elect not to reply to Dontrelle, but she forwards the email to other people—including the senior vice president—suggesting that Dontrelle must be struggling with his project. Danielle also declares, "I am highly confident I have the knowledge and experience required to develop the best solutions on my own." Dontrelle was not a recipient of Danielle's email.

At the end of six weeks, Dontrelle submits his special assignment recommendations to the senior vice president, and acknowledges the contributions of 11 people who supported the project. Danielle's recommendations are accompanied by a cover letter highlighting her pride in doing the entire project completely on her own.

The senior vice president asks you to be on the review committee that will evaluate Dontrelle's and Danielle's special assignment recommendations and provide them feedback. What insights might you share with them?

## Notes

_____

_____

_____

_____

_____

_____

_____

_____

_____

_____

_____

## Handling this Situation!

Dontrelle does reach out to Danielle in an effort to collaborate on this project, although he could have been more assertive about it. At least he recognizes that his best chance of being successful on the assignment is to deliver a useful set of recommendations and to develop them in a collaborative manner. He does a nice job of involving 11 other people and acknowledging their contributions.

Danielle may come up with excellent recommendations by working alone, but she clearly does not do a good job of understanding what the SVP wants. It's not only about *what* gets done, but *how* it gets done as well. And while she might succeed on this particular project going it alone, no one can do a big complex job successfully on an ongoing basis without working effectively with others. Danielle also makes a serious error in judgment by attempting to look good by disparaging Dontrelle to others behind his back. This strategy makes her appear petty and insecure, not to mention non-collaborative.

### Some additional advice for *WillBe*'s about Collaboration . . .

- Put the needs of the organization or team first, before your own.
- Ask people what you can do to help them, and then do it.
- Ask for help from others; it's a sign of strength not weakness.
- Collaborate with clear objectives in mind, not just for collaboration's sake.
- Embrace constructive conflict as a necessary condition for true collaboration.

## Self-Assessment

Mark the column that best describes your situation today.

| *Do I . . .* | Strength | Weakness | Not Sure |
|---|---|---|---|
| Put the organization's needs first? | _____ | _____ | _____ |
| Ask people how I can help them? | _____ | _____ | _____ |
| Ask for help from others? | _____ | _____ | _____ |
| Collaborate with clear objectives? | _____ | _____ | _____ |
| Embrace constructive conflict? | _____ | _____ | _____ |

## Actions I Will Take to Build on a Strength, Improve on a Weakness, and/or Learn More about Myself

_____

_____

_____

_____

_____

_____

_____

_____

_____

_____

_____

_____

# Chapter 6

## KEEP COMMON SENSE COMMON

*Watchword:* Judgment

THOMAS PAINE, ONE OF the fathers of the American Revolution, said, "The funny thing about common sense is that it's not that common." People with common sense have an innate ability to determine the appropriate course of action or reaction in a variety of circumstances. Quite simply, they have good judgment.

*WillBe*'s know how to handle tough situations and people, and possess a maturity beyond their years. They are unflappable during tough times, and project a sense of confidence without being arrogant. They **Keep Common Sense Common**.

They know when to act and when to watch, when to be assertive and when to stand back. They know when to talk and when to listen, when to lead and when to follow. They know how to push for what they want and when to compromise. They know how to win gratefully and how to lose graciously. Most importantly, they know how and when to make decisions, and when to wait for additional information and input before deciding.

What about intelligence? To be sure, a significant number of *WillBe*'s are very smart people. But a lot of individuals who never achieve their full potential are smart, too. Brain power is a great asset, yet it is not sufficient nor a firm requirement for success.

We all know really smart people who have absolutely no common sense. They remind us, however painfully, that intelligence does not necessarily equate to good judgment. *WillBe's* have the right blend of smarts and sense.

## A Situation!

Emma and Taylor have recently been hired from outside the company to lead complementary but separate video game development teams. As they are getting to know their new organizations, they discover an unorthodox and special talent who supports both of their teams, the chief creative consultant everyone refers to as "Stick." He's called Stick for two good reasons. First, no one seems to know his real name. Second, he is a virtuoso at joystick design and operation, so crucial to the video game experience.

Everyone on Emma's and Taylor's teams describe Stick as a brilliant visionary, and a lovable (most of the time) wacko. Emma and Taylor come to appreciate Stick for his ability to push people to think differently, and to develop elegant yet simple solutions to complex problems. He is both smart and practical.

They also learn the hard way that Stick is a contrarian who makes people uncomfortable, even as he causes them to be better video game designers. On balance, Emma and Taylor agree that Stick is a very valuable asset, despite some messiness. However, Taylor sees Stick as a treasure while Emma sees him as a necessary evil.

About three months into their new roles, Emma and Taylor have a meeting with their boss to discuss game development status and issues. At the conclusion of the meeting, their boss says, "You are both very fortunate to have great teams, with the exception of that weird guy—what's his name, Pogo?"

Emma and Taylor reply in unison, "You mean Stick?"

"Yeah, Stick," says their boss. "That guy makes me nervous. He seems like a loose cannon. What are you going to do about him?"

As Emma and Taylor leave their boss's office, they realize they have a tough decision to make. Do they push back on their boss to get him to appreciate Stick and his contributions better? Or do they use their boss's discomfort as an excuse to get rid of Stick?

Emma and Taylor debate the issue for several weeks. Emma knows Stick adds value, but is not sure whether it's worth fighting the boss over keeping him on the team. Taylor thinks Stick is worth the fight, but isn't sure they have all the information they need to make a firm decision.

You have worked with Stick and people like him before, so Emma and Taylor seek your views on what factors to consider. What do you think they should do?

## Notes

_____

_____

_____

_____

_____

_____

_____

_____

_____

_____

_____

## Handling this Situation!

Stick is a classic contrarian, who brings brilliant insights along with a lot of mess. The key question for Emma and Taylor is, "Do Stick's strengths outweigh his weaknesses?"

Everyone is a balance sheet, a combination of assets and liabilities. Emma and Taylor must make some judgments about whether Stick's assets exceed his liabilities or vice versa. They also need to ascertain why their boss feels so strongly about Stick and whether this opinion can be changed—and whether they are willing to put their judgment on the line to fight for Stick.

They probably have all the information they need about Stick at this point, except for whether he has the ability to modify his behavior just enough to address their boss's concerns. But they must first better understand their boss's reservations about Stick and whether they are accurate and fair. Only then can they determine whether any modification in Stick's style makes sense.

Emma and Taylor must learn not only what their boss thinks about Stick, but how he came to form those judgments. By the way, if it has occurred to you that life is not fair sometimes, you are correct. Emma and Taylor may discover that their boss does not like Stick for reasons that make no sense whatsoever, but they are still expected to do something about it. Once they understand their boss's issues with Stick better, they can begin working with Stick to help him modify his style without losing his creativity. Time will tell whether their efforts succeed.

### Some additional advice for *WillBe*'s about Judgment . . .

- Never allow your intelligence to substitute for good judgment.

- If you must choose between people with smarts or sense, pick sense.

- Pay attention to *how* people think, not just *what* they think.

- Keep a "free electron" or contrarian close to you; he or she will help you see things differently.

- Get comfortable making decisions without all the facts; it's how life works.

## Self-Assessment

Mark the column that best describes your situation today.

| *Do I . . .* | Strength | Weakness | Not Sure |
|---|---|---|---|
| Allow my intelligence to substitute for my good judgment? | _____ | _____ | _____ |
| Pick people with sense? | _____ | _____ | _____ |
| Pay attention to *how* people think? | _____ | _____ | _____ |
| Keep a contrarian close to me? | _____ | _____ | _____ |
| Make decisions without all the facts? | _____ | _____ | _____ |

**Actions I Will Take to Build on a Strength, Improve on a Weakness, and/or Learn More about Myself**

_____

_____

_____

_____

_____

_____

_____

_____

_____

_____

_____

_____

_____

_____

# Chapter 7

## SEE AROUND CORNERS

*Watchword:* Anticipation

MANAGEMENT GURU PETER DRUCKER, said, "The best way to predict the future is to create it." Much of the success of any society or organization can be traced to the ability of its people to anticipate future conditions, adapt, and survive.

True *WillBe's* have a very keen sense of what's coming next, the ability to **See Around Corners**. This sixth sense enables them to anticipate, predict, adapt, respond, and implement more quickly and accurately than others. It's a combination of asking great questions, knowing what signposts to look for, and doing the right things at critical inflection points.

Wayne Gretzky, hockey Hall of Famer said, "I do not skate to where the puck is, I skate to where it will be." That's anticipation.

The ability to anticipate is particularly critical to overall situational awareness. People who can see around corners understand what's coming at them from a variety of angles, and are especially sensitive to things not directly in front of them. They do a very effective job of integrating and processing a wide variety of inputs, and have uncanny insight about complex situations and relationships.

*WillBe's* often see patterns in seemingly unrelated things that others miss. Their skill at connecting the dots among data, situations, and people makes them adept at anticipating and acting quickly to address changing circumstances.

## A Situation!

Over the past six months, the early warning signs have begun to surface—declining sales, excess capacity across the industry, talk of pending economic woes, and investor pessimism. Li and Hans-Peter are having a heated debate about whether these trends signal a serious business downturn for their start-up company, or an opportunity to take market share from foundering competitors less prepared to handle the challenging times ahead.

Li declares, "We're not like everyone else. They are losers. We are winners." Hans-Peter counters with, "We have to pay attention to what's happening around us. If we misdiagnose what is going on, it may be too late for us to adjust our cost structure and recover quickly from a downturn."

Li is very visionary and aggressive, with a great understanding of the industry, but very stubborn and dismissive of competitors and industry analysts. Li believes in Li, relying on gut instincts and bravado to challenge and persuade others. Li is convinced she is right, despite mounting evidence and advice to the contrary. As a result, she continues to promote the company's growth prospects to customers, employees, and investors. Li thinks the world of Hans-Peter, but sometimes sees him as a wimp.

Hans-Peter is as equally experienced and visionary as Li, and is very optimistic about the company's long-term prospects. He really admires Li's confidence and commitment to winning, but sometimes worries she is so focused on being right that she misses important signals around her. Hans-Peter spends a lot of his time paying attention to economists' projections and industry forecasts—and talking to and listening to customers, suppliers, competitors, employees, and investors. He senses an impending downturn, and he wants the company to be ready to respond.

Since starting the company, Li and Hans-Peter rarely have time for anything but work. They decide to take a break, and invite you to play a round of golf with them. As you play, you make note of the irony—Li and Hans-Peter play golf like they run their business.

Li keeps her head down, attacks the ball without mercy, and doesn't spend much time surveying the greens before she putts. She scores well, almost willing the ball into the hole each time. Hans-Peter scans each fairway, takes a little longer than normal to select a club, and seems to enjoy the beauty of the course more than he enjoys keeping score. He plays a good round, observes that the weather is beginning to change for the worse, and recommends that the three of you head to the clubhouse for a drink.

Once settled at the bar, Li and Hans-Peter share with you the discussions they've been having about their start-up business's prospects and pending challenges. They request your insights on what may lie ahead. How can you assist them?

## Notes

_____

_____

_____

_____

_____

_____

_____

_____

_____

_____

_____

_____

## Handling this Situation!

Li is in a dangerous place—being really good, believing she and her company are really good, and failing to respect the capabilities and views of her competitors and other interested parties. It is extremely difficult to anticipate what is going to happen without paying attention to things and people around you. It would be like attempting to drive a car by looking only at your own dashboard, without ever looking up to see what the cars around you are doing, or what the weather and driving conditions are like.

Hans-Peter is the kind of person who considers the traffic patterns, roads, and weather conditions. Even if Li is not someone who pays much attention to these things, she needs a navigator who does pay attention. There is nothing wrong with having confidence in your point of view, as long as that confidence does not extend to completely ignoring the views of others. Arrogance is deadly to anticipation.

## Some additional advice for *WillBe*'s about Anticipation . . .

- Seek information from a diverse group of people about a wide variety of subjects, and look for patterns and themes.

- Ask a lot of questions about who, what, when, and how before asking why.

- Pay less attention to people's opinions than to how they arrive at those opinions.

- Find a hobby that allows you to clear your head; it's a great way to make room for unanticipated ideas, trends, and opportunities.

- Prepare as if you are right, but allow for the possibility you might be wrong.

## Self-Assessment

Mark the column that best describes your situation today.

| *Do I . . .* | Strength | Weakness | Not Sure |
|---|---|---|---|
| Seek information from diverse people? | ——— | ——— | ——— |
| Ask other questions before asking why? | ——— | ——— | ——— |
| Pay attention to how people arrive at their opinions? | ——— | ——— | ——— |
| Have a hobby that clears my head? | ——— | ——— | ——— |
| Allow for the possibility I might be wrong? | ——— | ——— | ——— |

## Actions I Will Take to Build on a Strength, Improve on a Weakness, and/or Learn More about Myself

————————————————————————

————————————————————————

————————————————————————

————————————————————————

————————————————————————

————————————————————————

————————————————————————

————————————————————————

————————————————————————

————————————————————————

# Chapter 8

## SPEND TIME LIKE MONEY

### *Watchword:* Prioritization

WOODY ALLEN SAID, "80% of success is just showing up." Perhaps another way to think about it might be that 100% of success is showing up in the right place, at the right time, for the right reasons, with the right approach.

In so many ways, presence equals priorities. People generally show up for things that are important to them—or to people they care about.

*WillBe's*, like the senior leaders they aspire to become, are being watched. Everyone wants to know "Where are they, what are they doing, and with whom are they spending time?" Answers to these questions provide important clues to one's priorities. They **Spend Time Like Money**, as if it were a precious commodity.

In an increasingly multitasking 24 x 7 world—where everyone is on stage all the time with YouTube, Twitter, Instant Messenger, and smart phones—knowing how to spend time on things that matter is an evaporating (yet essential) skill. Despite growing up in an attention deficit society, *WillBe's* know that how they spend their time says volumes about their priorities and their effectiveness. They align their time and effort around the things that matter most to their organization and to the people for whom and with whom they work.

*WillBe*'s master the paradox of competing priorities by doing a focused set of things extraordinarily well, rather than many more things in mediocre fashion. In addition, because they pay attention to the value of time, *WillBe*'s also show respect for other people's time. Most importantly, they align their passions with the things they do at work, at home, and at play.

## A Situation!

Morgan and Sasha are in highly visible leadership roles, with huge organizations and hundreds of people following their every move. They welcome the responsibility and actually enjoy the limelight, if not the constant demands on their time.

Morgan treats time like a commitment, while Sasha thinks of it as a commodity in plentiful supply. Morgan shows up when advertised, starts and ends meetings on time, and tries not to keep other people waiting around for guidance and feedback. Sasha promises to attend events, but often arrives unfashionably late or doesn't show at all, citing conflicts that are more important as an excuse. Meetings begin and end on "Sasha-time," and it is common for people to be kept waiting without explanation.

When invited to events and meetings that are important to others, Morgan jumps through hoops to be there and show support. Sasha attends if it's convenient. Morgan has a reputation as a leader whose priorities are the organization's priorities. Sasha is seen as one of those leaders whose priorities are his or her own. Morgan attempts to plan work such that people are not performing unnatural acts at the last minute to pull off miracles. Sasha seems to delight in keeping people in the dark until the eleventh hour, then expecting people to put forth Herculean efforts to save the day.

You are a peer of Morgan and Sasha, and are responsible for putting together an important conference. You need a well-regarded executive to serve as keynote speaker. Both Morgan and Sasha have expressed interest in serving in this capacity. They are awaiting your decision. Whom do you select and why?

## Notes

_____

_____

_____

_____

_____

_____

_____

_____

_____

_____

_____

## Handling this Situation!

If you don't respect other people's time, they will find it difficult to believe you respect them. Sasha seems to think that his time is more valuable than everyone else's time. Morgan goes out of her way to show support by being there for others.

Given a choice of which person to rely on, the decision should be easy. But this issue can quickly be extended to a discussion of the importance of prioritizing how we spend our time. The calendar is perhaps the most important and least understood tool an executive has. Virtually everyone is busy. That's not very useful or insightful. But try and answer this question, "Busy doing what?"

Understanding how time is being spent, on what things, when, and why provides key insight into what is important to us. Everyone is watching. Morgan seems to understand this reality more than Sasha and demonstrates she cares about the people and issues that are important to her. If you want others to believe they are important to you, be there when they need you and don't keep them waiting.

........................................................................................................

### Some additional advice for *WillBe*'s about Prioritization . . .

- Don't expect your sense of urgency to become someone else's emergency.

- Stop doing things that don't make sense to you and see if anyone notices.

- Review your calendar regularly in search of balance between thinking, creating, executing, building relationships, exercising, and having fun.

- Treat time—yours and other people's time—as precious.

- Spend time with the people you love, doing the things you love.

........................................................................................................

## Self-Assessment

Mark the column that best describes your situation today.

| *Do I . . .* | Strength | Weakness | Not Sure |
|---|---|---|---|
| Avoid confusing urgency with emergency? | _____ | _____ | _____ |
| Stop doing things that don't make sense? | _____ | _____ | _____ |
| Balance my calendar? | _____ | _____ | _____ |
| Treat time as precious? | _____ | _____ | _____ |
| Spend time with the people and things I love? | _____ | _____ | _____ |

## Actions I Will Take to Build on a Strength, Improve on a Weakness, and/or Learn More about Myself

_____

_____

_____

_____

_____

_____

_____

_____

_____

_____

_____

# Chapter 9

## FAIL FORWARD

*Watchword:* Resilience

THERE ARE THREE IMMUTABLE laws of failure:

1. Failure sucks.

2. Failure is, on occasion, inevitable.

3. Failure still sucks.

If we accept these laws as given, it becomes much easier for us to understand—not accept—failure. Then, failure can be channeled to help us reflect, rethink, reshape, respond, and rebound.

*WillBe's* exhibit remarkable resilience in the face of failure. They never seem to give up nor accept failure as defeat. They learn and grow from it, because they are incredibly active learners. They become stronger, because they are amazingly tough. They emerge better people, because they are better already.

*WillBe's* **Fail Forward** by using failure to propel them ahead to better ways of thinking and executing. To *WillBe's*, making mistakes and experiencing failure are both part of success. But just because *WillBe's* are rational about failure doesn't mean they like it.

## A Situation!

Hiroshi and Jordan are two well-regarded members of the leadership team. They occupy key positions with big responsibilities, and are seen by employees as representing all that is good about the organization's culture. Unfortunately for them, their boss had some significant strategic differences with the CEO and other members of the senior leadership team, and recently left the company.

Their new boss has arrived with an agenda to change the culture, and has a bias for surrounding himself with people he already knows and has worked with before. As a result of this leadership and philosophy change, Hiroshi and Jordan have very similar conversations with their new boss, who tells each of them separately, "The company genuinely appreciates your past contributions, but we are going to be making some changes, including with the position you now hold. We have prepared a very fair separation package for you and wish you well."

Needless to say, neither Hiroshi nor Jordan is thrilled with their dismissals, which they see as arbitrary and unfair—especially in light of all they have done for the company. However, the way each chooses to handle the setback varies considerably.

Hiroshi recognizes that life is not always fair, acts like a complete professional, takes the high road, and refuses to badmouth the new leader or the company. He learns from the experience, puts together a great resume and networking strategy, and looks forward with confidence and optimism. Within a few months, he has a number of potential job prospects that look great and offer higher pay.

Jordan goes ballistic and decides to criticize the new leader and company publicly, despite signing a severance agreement preventing him from making disparaging remarks. Even during interviews for new jobs, he cannot resist the temptation to trash his former company and complain about how he was treated. Jordan can't help taking the decision to release him personally, and he spends a few months very angry and depressed.

Despite Jordan's excellent qualifications, several prospective employers decline to make him a job offer based on their concerns about his negative attitude. He is having difficulty finding a job, and the few prospects he has identified offer less responsibility and pay than he is willing to accept.

As part of their job search networking activities, Hiroshi and Jordan approach you for recommendations. What do you suggest to them?

## Notes

_____

_____

_____

_____

_____

_____

_____

_____

_____

_____

_____

## Handling this Situation!

Failure does not always require somebody to do something wrong. More often than not, people are doing their best and are well-intentioned, but sometimes things simply don't turn out the way they want.

Failure does not always have to be a referendum on you as a person. However, how you handle failure is always a reflection on you. Hiroshi handles things in a mature fashion, makes the best of a difficult situation, and ends up looking like a winner. Jordan goes crazy and probably feels great about criticizing others—momentarily. However, after the emotion subsides, reality sets in.

Not only has Jordan had to endure an unpleasant experience, he looks bad while going through it. If you are going to get worked up about failure, focus on resilience and optimism rather than on anger and bitterness. People will feel good about you, and so will you.

........................................................................................................................

### Some additional advice for *WillBe*'s about Resilience . . .

- Treat failure as a temporary delay in gratification, not a permanent state of being.

- Reflect on failure long enough to learn from it, but not long enough to become comfortable with it.

- Recognize that you cannot always control what happens to you, but you can control how you respond to it.

- Recover from failure quickly and constructively; people will be watching how you handle yourself.

- Be humble. Life is a series of near failures, periodically interrupted by random acts of success.

........................................................................................................................

## Self-Assessment

Mark the column that best describes your situation today.

| *Do I . . .* | Strength | Weakness | Not Sure |
|---|---|---|---|
| Treat failure as a temporary delay in gratification? | ———— | ———— | ———— |
| Learn from failure? | ———— | ———— | ———— |
| Control how I respond to failure? | ———— | ———— | ———— |
| Recover quickly and constructively? | ———— | ———— | ———— |
| Maintain humility? | ———— | ———— | ———— |

## Actions I Will Take to Build on a Strength, Improve on a Weakness, and/or Learn More about Myself

_____

_____

_____

_____

_____

_____

_____

_____

_____

_____

_____

_____

_____

# Chapter 10

## FILL THE VOID

*Watchword:* Responsibility

MANY YEARS AGO, I received a great piece of career advice, "The best way to make a contribution is to find a void and fill it. Look for problems no one is solving, those things that need fixing that no one else is fixing. Take responsibility for things that no one else will."

That's what *WillBe*'s do, they **Fill the Void** by taking responsibility, even when they don't or shouldn't have to. *WillBe*'s know the secret to figuring out where to start and what to fix. They ask.

People may not always be able to describe the root cause of problems, but they will always know what gets in their way and what frustrates them. *WillBe*'s are very good at finding out what gets in people's way.

It's not uncommon to hear *WannaBe*'s say, "Someone should really do something about that . . . " *WillBe*'s are that "someone."

Yet, despite their willingness to take responsibility, *WillBe*'s do not overdo it by exhibiting blind ambition. They don't lobby for other people's jobs, nor do they inappropriately criticize others to create opportunities for themselves.

Many organizations make heroes out of firefighters, those people who rush to the rescue to resolve crises. All too often, these *WannaBe*'s are the ones who started the fire in the first place. What better way to appear indispensable later?

*WillBe*'s are clearly valuable, but for more constructive reasons. They bring positive solutions, coupled with a genuine willingness to assist by filling the void left by others.

## A Situation!

Bryce and Cole, marketing department heads, transfer into a new division as part of a major business acquisition, integration, and reorganization. They are looking forward to being part of the new organization, yet are also fearful that their former company's identity and ways of doing business will be destroyed as part of what they see as a "takeover."

Most employees in their departments are nervous and negative about impending changes and what those changes might mean to them. Everyone feels that the acquiring company, Evil Empire Enterprises, is doing a terrible job communicating information and status regarding the acquisition integration.

Bryce and Cole are growing increasingly frustrated because their team members are coming to them with questions they cannot answer. Bryce feels undermined because he looks like he doesn't know what's going on. Cole feels helpless because he wants to be able to provide better information to his people.

Bryce sits in staff meetings with his arms folded and joins with other employees in openly and regularly criticizing Evil Empire Enterprises for doing such a poor job of keeping employees informed. He feels like a victim, and acts like one.

Cole is frustrated too, but decides to find out what he can do to improve the situation. He meets with the leader of the integration process and discovers the communications team is overwhelmed with competing priorities, further complicated by one team member taking an unexpected medical leave of absence. They need help.

Cole volunteers to bring small groups of employees together to generate lists of questions about the acquisition. He agrees to pass them along to the integration team and to assist in drafting answers. Cole also assigns his marketing communications manager to the integration team on a temporary basis, to update and manage the weekly postings on the integration Web site.

When the integration process is completed four months later, Bryce's and Cole's departments are combined into one. The selection committee that will interview candidates for the new marketing department head position is meeting in one week.

In advance of their interviews, both Bryce and Cole individually seek your coaching on how to handle the interview process, including what you think will be emphasized. What do you tell them?

## Notes

_____

_____

_____

_____

_____

_____

_____

_____

_____

_____

_____

## Handling this Situation!

Frustration almost always leads to action. The issue is, what kind of action—productive or non-productive?

Bryce allows his frustration to take him into a negative spiral, and he actually becomes part of the problem. Cole is frustrated too, but channels his energy in a constructive manner and becomes part of the solution.

People who can identify problems are in plentiful supply. Those who can see solutions as well as problems are worth their weight in gold. If you spend a lot of time thinking to yourself, "It's not my problem," you are a problem. Spend time thinking, "How can I help fix this problem?" Then, take responsibility and action.

### Some additional advice for *WillBe*'s about Responsibility . . .

- Take responsibility rather than waiting for someone to give it to you.
- Find a void and fill it.
- Own the problem, and don't make excuses.
- Take the blame, share the glory.
- Don't wait for divine organizational guidance from above, control your own destiny.

## Self-Assessment

Mark the column that best describes your situation today.

| *Do I . . .* | Strength | Weakness | Not Sure |
|---|---|---|---|
| Take responsibility? | _____ | _____ | _____ |
| Fill the void? | _____ | _____ | _____ |
| Own the problem without excuses? | _____ | _____ | _____ |
| Take the blame and share the glory? | _____ | _____ | _____ |
| Control my own destiny? | _____ | _____ | _____ |

## Actions I Will Take to Build on a Strength, Improve on a Weakness, and/or Learn More about Myself

_____

_____

_____

_____

_____

_____

_____

_____

_____

_____

_____

_____

_____

# Chapter 11

## SEEK THE TRUTH

*Watchword:* Communication

GEORGE BERNARD SHAW SAID, "The biggest problem with communication is the illusion that it has taken place." Leaders of any organization have a huge challenge in promoting an environment of openness, candor, trust, and inclusion. We often think of people who are great communicators as those who are effective or even dynamic speakers and presenters, people who can tell a story with flair and charisma.

To be sure, "telling" skills are very conducive to communication, but they do not distinguish truly great communicators. The best communicators are first and foremost great listeners.

*WillBe's* have a way of making people comfortable about telling them things. They actively and regularly **Seek the Truth** by soliciting input and ideas from a diverse set of people. They also use their knowledge of what's really going on to provide candid, constructive feedback to others who can benefit from the truth and do something about it. Not only do they seek the truth, they promote, encourage, foster, and embrace it. Ron Sugar, the great retired chairman and CEO of Northrop Grumman, used to say, "We want good news to travel fast, and bad news to travel even faster."

*WannaBe's* are often noticed in organizations solely because they can deliver great presentations. *WillBe's* are the people everyone wants to talk to for advice well before and after the PowerPoint puppet show, when the real work gets done.

## A Situation!

Chris and Sam are team leaders in a small company who receive a very troubling letter from eight employees, four in each of their departments. The letter, signed by the employees, details a list of complaints and accusations against a very senior and powerful executive involving potential abuse of power and possible conflicts of interest with a key supplier.

Chris and Sam are determined to get to the bottom of the accusations, but are also highly attuned to the political ramifications of making the accused senior executive look bad. They discuss the situation and agree to meet with their employees.

During the individual one-on-one interviews with their respective employees, Sam listens actively and attentively without interruption. She asks clarifying questions and summarizes what is being said to ensure understanding. She tries hard not to pass judgment on the accusations or debate the merits of each employee's feelings. At the conclusion of each interview, Sam thanks each person for having the courage to come forward with his or her concerns, and promises to bring closure to the issues quickly and fairly. Her employees seem to leave the discussions feeling heard, although still nervous and somewhat skeptical about what will happen next.

Chris' interviews go a little differently. In an attempt to convince his employees that their claims are exaggerated, he spends most of the time talking instead of listening. Chris is very skeptical about the accusations, which makes it difficult for him to hear what employees are trying to tell him. Recognizing that Chris isn't really listening, his interviewees do their best to express their concerns, but lightly skim over some of the more serious perceived abuses for fear of reprisals. Chris completes each meeting satisfied that he is able to discern fact from fiction, while his employees all leave feeling very uncomfortable and wondering whether they should have raised their concerns in the first place.

Following the interviews, Chris and Sam get together to compare notes about what they learned. Not surprisingly, Chris feels the accusations are exaggerated and not that serious. Furthermore, he expresses concern over angering the accused senior executive with negative feedback. Therefore, he thinks the issue should be dropped. Sam feels the complaints are not as serious as she originally thought, but that they still need to be dealt with immediately. Sam believes both the accused executive and the employees who made the accusations deserve feedback to minimize any misperceptions and misunderstandings in the future.

Chris and Sam continue to discuss next steps and agree you would lend a useful perspective to the situation. They seek your counsel about how to handle the follow up with the employees and the accused senior leader. What do you recommend?

## Notes

_____

_____

_____

_____

_____

_____

_____

_____

_____

_____

_____

_____

## Handling this Situation!

When I was a child, my father would sometimes tell me sternly, "Don't do as I do, do as I say." Of course, he found it difficult to keep a straight face because he realized the futility of what he was asking.

People pay much more attention to what we do—our behavior and non-verbal cues—than to our words. We often confuse communication with talking and telling, rather than focusing on much more important factors such as listening and being present.

Chris tells his employees he wants to hear what they have to say about the executive's questionable behavior, but everything he does and says after that leads his people to conclude he's not really willing to listen. Sam demonstrates her willingness to listen to her team, but even then, they are worried and skeptical about what will happen next.

Assume that people disbelieve you before they believe you, and don't really hear you until they really hear you. Repeating the message, ensuring consistency between message and behavior, listening to people on their home turf where they feel safer, and playing back to them what you heard them say are all techniques that improve your chances of fostering effective communication.

To put this issue to bed effectively, the accused executive and accusing employees both need to know what Chris and Sam heard, and how the situation will be remedied going forward. The loop must be closed.

**Some additional advice for *WillBe's* about Communication . . .**

- Improve communication by listening more than talking.
- Make it safe for people to tell you what they think.
- Be transparent with others about what you believe and why.
- Provide candid feedback and actively check for understanding.
- Cherish the truth, especially when it hurts; it's your friend.

## Self-Assessment

Mark the column that best describes your situation today.

| *Do I . . .* | Strength | Weakness | Not Sure |
|---|---|---|---|
| Listen more than I talk? | _____ | _____ | _____ |
| Make it safe for people to tell me? | _____ | _____ | _____ |
| Tell people what I believe and why? | _____ | _____ | _____ |
| Provide candid feedback? | _____ | _____ | _____ |
| Cherish the truth? | _____ | _____ | _____ |

**Actions I Will Take to Build on a Strength, Improve on a Weakness, and/or Learn More about Myself**

_____

_____

_____

_____

_____

_____

_____

_____

_____

_____

_____

_____

_____

_____

# Chapter 12

## KNOW THYSELF

*Watchword:* Self-Awareness

MY OLDEST SON BOUGHT me a T-shirt with a great quote on the back, "I married my wife for her looks, but not the ones she's been giving me lately." That sums up self-awareness to me.

Do people understand what motivates them, what they like and dislike, what they are good at and not so good at, and most importantly, what impact they have on others?

If not, they are probably like many others, blissfully oblivious.

*WillBe's* adhere to the adage, **Know Thyself**, and are objective about their strengths, weaknesses, priorities, motivations, and effect on other people. They actively seek feedback—formally and informally—and spend more time trying to critique their own developmental needs constructively than they do convincing themselves and others how great they are.

*WillBe's* actually like knowing where they stand, love acting on input and advice, and use their self-awareness as fuel for taking control of and managing their own careers.

Most importantly, *WillBe's* know how to have fun, laugh at themselves, and not take themselves too seriously. Believe it or not, people often see others with a sense of humor and humility as being more human. Imagine that.

## A Situation!

Hakeem and JJ are honored to be invited to a leadership development program for high potentials along with 30 of their peers from across the company. The program, called ELITE (Executive Leadership Institute for Talented Egomaniacs), is a weeklong experience at an offsite location, with faculty consisting of internal senior leaders and external experts. Topics include strategy, financial acumen, leadership and personal development, and external economic and public policy trends, among other things.

After receiving all the pre-work for ELITE, Hakeem and JJ notice a significant portion of the program will be devoted to better understanding their own leadership styles and behaviors, receiving 360 degree feedback, and putting in place action plans to address their development needs or "flat spots." Hakeem's first thought is, "This leadership feedback will probably be helpful, if it doesn't get me fired first." JJ's first thought is, "This feedback will be a piece of cake. I got all 'A's in college and graduate school, how hard can this be?"

Weeks later, Hakeem's and JJ's preparations for ELITE have been completed, including soliciting 360 degree feedback inputs from their boss, peers, direct reports, and other colleagues. During day two of ELITE, their soon-to-be feedback coaches hand each of them a sealed envelope containing their personal feedback report. Hakeem is thinking about the time he got a "D" in penmanship in the sixth grade and his hands start to sweat. JJ is thinking about what he is going to have for lunch from the hotel's very generous buffet.

Following a thorough review of their reports, both Hakeem and JJ experience barely perceptible numbness in their faces and dull ringing in their ears. As they refocus on what their reports actually say, a few themes emerge that are remarkably similar for both of them: strengths—extremely bright, passionate, strategic, decisive, and assertive; development needs—a little too arrogant and self-assured, impatient, and naïve about what it takes to get things done in this culture.

Both of them receive very similar scores and written comments, including one comment that is exactly the same and looks to be written by the same person, "You have a huge brain and enormous potential. There is no need for you to let people know how smart and great you are. Everyone already knows, but it sounds arrogant coming from you. Tone it down and you will find people are very supportive of you."

For Hakeem, the positive feedback feels great and the negative feedback is a painful yet helpful eye-opener. He even laughs a bit and tries not to take himself too seriously. For JJ, the negative feedback is embarrassing and insulting, and all the positive feedback gets lost amid his defensiveness and anger. Hakeem begins working on his action plan. JJ spends most of his time trying to figure out who made the negative comments.

You are a fellow participant in the ELITE program. After reviewing your own feedback, Hakeem and JJ turn to you and inquire about your feedback, how you plan to address it, and whether you have any suggestions for them. What do you say?

## Notes

_____

_____

_____

_____

_____

_____

_____

_____

_____

_____

_____

## Handling this Situation!

No one really likes to receive negative feedback or to be criticized. Some people just handle it better than others do.

Assume the following: Hakeem is not perfect, JJ is not perfect, and you are not perfect. Everyone sees our strengths and weaknesses—they have to live with us every day. Others do not judge us by how perfect we are, they judge us by how perfectly we deal with our imperfections. Ask for feedback. Act on it. Give others feedback. Help them act on it. Lighten up a little. Lather. Rinse. Repeat.

............................................................................................................................

### Some additional advice for *WillBe*'s about Self-Awareness . . .

- Solicit feedback on your strengths, weaknesses, and interpersonal style.

- Acknowledge your development needs and give people permission to help you address them.

- Give constructive feedback to others; it improves your chances of getting the same in return.

- Get 360 degree feedback every 18 to 24 months, and assess your progress.

- Openly admit you are not perfect; everyone else around you already knows.

............................................................................................................................

## Self-Assessment

Mark the column that best describes your situation today.

| *Do I . . .* | Strength | Weakness | Not Sure |
|---|---|---|---|
| Solicit feedback? | _____ | _____ | _____ |
| Acknowledge my development needs? | _____ | _____ | _____ |
| Give constructive feedback? | _____ | _____ | _____ |
| Get 360 degree feedback? | _____ | _____ | _____ |
| Admit that I am not perfect? | _____ | _____ | _____ |

## Actions I Will Take to Build on a Strength, Improve on a Weakness, and/or Learn More about Myself

_____

_____

_____

_____

_____

_____

_____

_____

_____

_____

_____

_____

_____

_____

# Chapter 13

## DO WINDOWS

*Watchword:* Execution

A WISE MENTOR ONCE told me, "One's past track record is the best predictor of future success." There is no substitute for working hard, executing well, and delivering great results. Period.

One of the big fallacies of being a WillBe is that people tend to think primarily in terms of the future. Hence, the term "WillBe." In reality, being a WillBe starts with the past and the present—being an "AlreadyAre."

*WillBe's* already are well-regarded excellent performers who are not reluctant to roll up their sleeves and do real work—the hard stuff. They **Do Windows**, and they do them well.

Over time, *WillBe's* are given more difficult and important windows to clean, on progressively higher floors, in increasingly difficult places to reach, in bigger and more complex buildings. But they never forget how to do windows. Success for *WillBe's* begins and ends with execution . . . and clean windows.

### A Situation!

Kiley and Riley have been best friends since Kindergarten. They grew up next door to one another. After college, they started work on the same day—Kiley with a manufacturing and technology company and Riley with a consulting and professional services company. After seven years, both are now managers and anxious to be promoted to positions of bigger responsibility. They root for one another's success and compare notes constantly on career successes, frustrations, and lessons learned.

One Saturday morning, they are talking over coffee at the local CaffeineScene, doing some heavy self-reflection about their lives and career accomplishments. They ask questions such as, "Have we done the right things?" "Have we done enough?" "What could we be doing better?" And "What's missing?"

Deeply engrossed in their conversation, they don't notice you walking into CaffeineScene with your supersized travel mug and laptop in hand. You see Kiley and Riley first, and wander over to say hello after filling your mug with today's special blend, "LattaNuttin."

You grew up down the street from Kiley and Riley, and were six years ahead of them in school. But you know them and their families well, and they have always looked up to you for wisdom and advice—as if you represent a sneak preview of what their lives will be like in the future.

They quickly fill you in on their conversation and reflections, and you smile. They say, "What's so amusing?" You reply, "Not amusing, amazing."

You then proceed to tell them about a project you have been working on at the office that addresses this very subject. They excitedly ask you to share more. As you open your laptop, Kiley and Riley lean forward, interested to see what appears on your computer screen. Emerging from the screen's darkness, the following list bursts into view:

# WillBe Checklist

*Do you . . .*

1. **Define the Moments** by understanding that ethics and integrity are foundational to everything else?

2. **Do Unto Others** by treating everyone with dignity and respect?

3. **Show and Tell** by doing what you say you will do?

4. **Bring Out the Best** by causing others to want to be better?

5. **Play Sandbox** by willingly sharing ideas, resources, and people across boundaries?

6. **Keep Common Sense Common** by having good judgment and knowing when to act and when to stand back?

7. **See Around Corners** by having a keen sense of what's coming next, and an ability to anticipate, predict, adapt, respond, and implement?

8. **Spend Time Like Money** by reconciling competing priorities and focusing on people and things that matter most?

9. **Fail Forward** by treating failure as a temporary delay in gratification, not a permanent state of being?

10. **Fill the Void** by looking for problems no one else is fixing and taking responsibility for fixing them?

11. **Seek the Truth** by communicating in ways that show you are transparent and approachable?

12. **Know Thyself** by understanding your strengths, weaknesses, and impact on other people?

13. **Do Windows** by executing well and delivering great results?

## Are You a WillBe or a WannaBe???

Kiley and Riley stare at the computer screen for a minute or two, but it seems much longer. Suddenly, all the years of being best friends take over. Kiley shouts, "Riley, I think you're a WillBe!" Riley exclaims in unison, "Kiley, I think you're a WillBe!"

Either the caffeine is now taking full effect, or they feel quite good about themselves, their lives, and their careers.

As the euphoria subsides momentarily, they revisit the list and inquire about the last item, "Do Windows," and ask you to describe that one in more detail.

"It's very simple, but crucial," you reply. "Work hard, do the difficult things no one else wants to do, and make great things happen. It's nearly impossible to do all the other things on the list if you don't 'Do Windows,' and it's even harder to 'Do Windows' without doing all the other things on the list."

"Got it," say Kiley and Riley.

Then they ask you the toughest question of all, "When is a WillBe not a WillBe?" What do you reply?*

..............................................................................................................

*See Appendix G for the answer

## Notes

_____

_____

_____

_____

_____

_____

_____

_____

_____

_____

## Handling this Situation!

At the end of the day, nothing matters without performance and results. Execution is about getting results.

Some people believe that, as long as you deliver results, it doesn't matter how you achieve them. There are no style points. Others argue that results count, but not unless your behavior and operating style are also first class.

Here's the dilemma. It's much easier to assess quantitative results objectively than qualitative results. And it is infinitely easier to agree on what qualifies as negative behavior versus positive behavior.

So the surest path to failure is bad results combined with bad behavior, but does it follow that the surest path to success is great results combined with great behavior? Perhaps, but only if you understand what constitutes great results and behavior.

It is risky business to assume your definition of greatness is the right definition. How do you know? Try doing what Kiley and Riley do: **ask**.

........................................................................................

**Some additional advice for *WillBe*'s about Execution . . .**

- Do the difficult jobs, not just the glamorous ones.

- Help others with their tough jobs, they will be forever grateful.

- Be a high performer as a pre-requisite to becoming a high potential.

- Clarify up front what great performance looks like, so you don't have to brag about it when you deliver.

- Work harder than required, not as a substitute for but as a multiplier to great results.

........................................................................................

## Self-Assessment

Mark the column that best describes your situation today.

| *Do I . . .* | Strength | Weakness | Not Sure |
|---|---|---|---|
| Do the difficult jobs? | ____ | ____ | ____ |
| Help others with their tough jobs? | ____ | ____ | ____ |
| Perform at a high level? | ____ | ____ | ____ |
| Clarify what great performance is? | ____ | ____ | ____ |
| Work harder than required? | ____ | ____ | ____ |

## Actions I Will Take to Build on a Strength, Improve on a Weakness, and/or Learn More about Myself

_____

_____

_____

_____

_____

_____

_____

_____

_____

_____

_____

_____

_____

# Epilogue

SIR ISAAC NEWTON'S THIRD Law of Motion states that, "For every action, there is an equal and opposite reaction." This attempt to explain Physics could just as easily have been an effort to explain personal change. For every change you try to make in yourself, there are equally compelling forces fighting against the change. It's too hard. It's going to take too long. It's uncomfortable. It's risky. It's too costly. It's no fun. It's just not who I am.

The message of this book is not "change yourself." It is "be yourself."

If you did the math, you figured out that the book highlights 13 behaviors, each one further detailed into five pieces of advice for *WillBe's*. That is 65 things to be good at, not including your own list of things that are important to you.

AT THE RISK OF SERIOUS INJURY, DO NOT TRY THIS AT HOME.

Do not attempt to be equally great—or even better—at 65 things. Be aware of these behaviors and use them as a roadmap for the journey to understanding what highly effective *WillBe's* do. But, do not try to be someone you are not.

These behaviors have not all been displayed by the same WillBe at the same time under the same circumstances. Pick a few things you are great at and build on those strengths, or identify several weaknesses you have and improve on them—or find some things about yourself you would like to better understand, and figure them out.

Several appendices follow to help you review the **WillBe Checklist** and make some lists of your own. The rest of the book is food for thought and can be used for future reference, after you have made progress on your more immediate priorities.

Remember . . . the best thing about *WillBe's* is that they are who they are in a world that is what it is.

# WillBe Checklist

*Do you . . .*

1.  **Define the Moments** by understanding that ethics and integrity are foundational to everything else?

2.  **Do Unto Others** by treating everyone with dignity and respect?

3.  **Show and Tell** by doing what you say you will do?

4.  **Bring Out the Best** by causing others to want to be better?

5.  **Play Sandbox** by willingly sharing ideas, resources, and people across boundaries?

6.  **Keep Common Sense Common** by having good judgment and knowing when to act and when to stand back?

7.  **See Around Corners** by having a keen sense of what's coming next, and an ability to anticipate, predict, adapt, respond, and implement?

8.  **Spend Time Like Money** by reconciling competing priorities and focusing on people and things that matter most?

9.  **Fail Forward** by treating failure as a temporary delay in gratification, not a permanent state of being?

10. **Fill the Void** by looking for problems no one else is fixing and taking responsibility for fixing them?

11. **Seek the Truth** by communicating in ways that show you are transparent and approachable?

12. **Know Thyself** by understanding your strengths, weaknesses, and impact on other people?

13. **Do Windows** by executing well and delivering great results?

## Are You a WillBe or a WannaBe???

# 1 to 3 Highest Priority Actions I Will Take to Build on a Strength, Improve on a Weakness, and/or Learn More about Myself

_____

_____

_____

_____

_____

_____

_____

_____

_____

_____

_____

_____

_____

_____

_____

_____

_____

_____

**Additional Notes:**

# How's My Progress on the Top 1 to 3 Actions I Committed to Address?

_____

_____

_____

_____

_____

_____

_____

_____

_____

_____

_____

_____

_____

_____

_____

_____

_____

_____

_____

**Additional Notes:**

## How's My Progress on the Top 1 to 3 Actions I Committed to Address?

_____

_____

_____

_____

_____

_____

_____

_____

_____

_____

_____

_____

_____

_____

_____

_____

_____

_____

_____

_____

_____

**Additional Notes:**

## How's My Progress on the Top 1 to 3 Actions I Committed to Address?

_____

_____

_____

_____

_____

_____

_____

_____

_____

_____

_____

_____

_____

_____

_____

_____

_____

_____

_____

_____

_____

_____

**Additional Notes:**

## How's My Progress on the Top 1 to 3 Actions I Committed to Address? Is there Anything Else I Should Begin to Address?

_____

_____

_____

_____

_____

_____

_____

_____

_____

_____

_____

_____

_____

_____

_____

_____

_____

_____

_____

_____

_____

_____

_____

_____

**Additional Notes:**

***Answer to Question from Chapter 13***

## When is a WillBe not a WillBe?

*ANSWER:* When you are sure you have become one—because once you are sure you are a WillBe, you run the risk of no longer developing yourself and getting better. Complacency and cockiness are for *WannaBe's*, not *WillBe's*. Enjoy who you are, be proud of what you have achieved, but don't lose the passion to improve—that's what makes you special.

# Acknowledgments

I WOULD LIKE TO thank Lee Dyer of Cornell University, John Boudreau and Ed Lawler of the University of Southern California, Barry Posner of Santa Clara University, and Dave Ulrich of the University of Michigan and the RBL Group for their very helpful and encouraging comments and advice as they reviewed early drafts of this book.

Special thanks go to Harriet Edwards for her editing support, as well as to Matt McGovern for his expertise with the final editing and publishing process. In addition, insightful comments from Heather Laychak, Jennifer McEwen, and Will Sproule added immeasurably to the final product.

My sincere gratitude to career mentors and advisors including Howard Knicely, Bill Maltarich, and Ron Sugar for believing in me. I also wish to express my admiration and affection for the HR leaders and team members at TRW, Qwest Communications, and Northrop Grumman. I learned so much about commitment, caring, and courage from all of you. In particular, my special thanks go to executive assistants Debbie Metsch, Terri Carrigan, and Laura Barreda for their remarkable dedication in endeavoring to make me look a lot better than I really am.

Likewise, I would like to acknowledge the many peer and up-and-coming leaders from my own companies as well as other organizations—you brought out the best in me. And, to the faculty, staff, and students of Binghamton University, Cornell University, and the University of Southern California . . . thanks for everything you do to invest in the development of others, including me.

Finally, I offer my love and appreciation to my family and friends—especially my wife Susan Edwards and our children Tyler, Eric, and Matthew Ziskin; my mother and father, Marilyn and Ted Ziskin, and my brother, Adam Ziskin; as well as all the extended members of the Edwards, Glasser, and MacLellan clans who provide a constant source of inspiration and support.

# About the Author

IAN ZISKIN IS PRESIDENT of **EXec EXcel Group LLC**, a human capital consulting firm he founded following a highly successful 28 year career as a business executive.

Ian is also Executive in Residence to Cornell University's Center for Advanced Human Resource Studies (CAHRS) at the School of Industrial and Labor Relations, as well as to USC's Center for Effective Organizations (CEO) at the Marshall School of Business. Previously, Ian served in Chief Human Resources Officer and other senior roles with three Fortune 100 corporations: Northrop Grumman, Qwest Communications, and TRW.

Ian has a Master of Industrial and Labor Relations degree from Cornell University and a Bachelor of Science degree in Management from Binghamton University, where he graduated magna cum laude.

In 2007, Ian was elected a Fellow of the National Academy of Human Resources, considered the highest honor in the HR profession.

For additional information on the author and **EXec EXcel Group**, visit www.exexgroup.com.